MULL HIGHLAND GAMES: THE CENTENARY

Eric Macintyre

PUBLISHED BY MULL HIGHLAND GAMES SCIO

www.mullhighlandgames.com

Paperback and digital edition produced in 2023

Cover image: Jay Scott putting the shot.

Acknowledgements

Many people have provided help, advice, memories and photos to help produce this work and I would like to thank them. They include: Andrew Kain, Robert MacLeod, Avril Macintyre, Mary Macintyre, Florence Kirsop, Dr Lorn Macintyre, the late Brigadier John Macfarlane, Alistair MacNeill, Katriona Lloyd, Jean Swanston, Anna Eifert, Susan Windram, Callum MacLachlainn, Gordon Grant, Fergie MacDonald, Iona MacLean, Morag MacDonald, Carol Anne Harris, Bill MacCallum, Olive Brown, Georgia Satchel, Archivist at Mull Museum. But most of all I would like to thank my late mother Betty for diligently putting Games programmes and Oban Times cuttings in that drawer for so many years, thereby providing me with so much material for this book. My apologies if I have missed anyone out, but I thank you all the same.

Eric Macintyre, March 2023

ERIC MACINTYRE

Foreword

I feel very honoured to be asked to write the foreword for this fascinating book put together by Eric Macintyre to commemorate the 100 years of the Mull Highland Games. The author has managed to gather much information about the first century of the Games and as he says in his acknowledgements, much of that information came from his mother's records that she kept of the Games over many years. The Mull Highland Games have always been known as the Friendly Games and the Local Games. It was never that easy for some of the international competitors to get to Mull, so many of the sporting events were dominated by local athletes. They were seen as the friendly Games because everyone competing was always applauded, and the late Ronnie Campbell who was the announcer at the Games for many years, always encouraged the crowds to support the man who came last just as much as the winner. The view from the natural grandstand can't be beaten by anywhere else in Scotland, looking down the Sound of Mull. Originally many boats came from Coll, Tiree, Lochaline and Ardnamurchan to bring people to the Games as well as the King George that would call in on its way to Staffa and Iona with another huge crowd of people. With over 3,500 people attending, it was a great day out for many people who were working very hard during the year.

Eric describes marching up the hill to the Games ground, which seems to get harder as I get older, but I always remember that the City of Glasgow Police Band was, I think, the only band that played non-stop up to the Games ground. What a magnificent band they were, and they have been followed by many other bands including Angus MacColl and the Oban High School Pipe Band who have played us up the hill for several years now.

There have been many famous athletes who have performed at Tobermory. I remember in particular the Scott brothers from Inchmurrin on Loch Lomond, and Bill Anderson the heavyweight champion of Scotland who for many years fought off professional heavyweights who came north to play on the Games circuit.

Finally, the Tobermory Games have been run by a nucleus of several families for many years. The Kains, the MacLeods from the Mishnish and the Macintyre family itself have all given great service to the Games. The other group of helpers who must not be forgotten are those who volunteer to get the ground ready every year, and who work so hard to make it look so nice. There can't be many Games where the landing pit for the long-jump is the bunker outside the ninth hole of a golf course.

I am sure you will enjoy Eric's book as much as I have.

Lachlan Maclean of Duart

ERIC MACINTYRE

Introduction

Mull Highland Games has played an important part in the life of Mull and surrounding areas for a century and as we celebrate that centenary, it is fitting to look back at how the Games have changed and adapted over the years. This is not a full history of everything that has happened over those 100 years. Rather, it tries to give a chronicle of the major events of past decades, as well as featuring some of the great characters, both competitors and officials, who have made Mull Highland Games what they still are today, a vital annual celebration for all the community. Not all of these characters can be included in this work, so apology must be made for any omissions of people or events. This is entirely the responsibility of the author.

ERIC MACINTYRE

Highland Games In Scottish History

Highland Games have been held in Scotland for hundreds, if not thousands, of years. Mull Highland Games have been part of that tradition for nearly 150 years. It is impossible to put exact dates on the origins of the sporting and other contests which make up a modern Highland Games, but some general observations are in order. Feats of strength are likely to have been contested in small, rural settlements long before towns became established; and foot racing up hills and mountains is an ancient tradition. As the Highland aristocratic families took on personal pipers, such as the legendary MacCrimmons in Skye, so traditions and tunes for the pipes became established, leading on to competitions. In the same way,castles and mansions would have been the source of many dances which later became more popular. Over time these activities would come together in annual events which might be linked to religious festivals or the few holidays which people enjoyed in the past.

We can date some events more certainly than others. Ceres in Fife lays claim to being the oldest Games in Scotland having first being held in 1314 as archers returned from the Battle of Bannockburn. Over the next centuries many events sprung up all over Scotland and the traditions and events really came together in the 19thcentury. The St Fillans Games were first held in 1819, and perhaps the most famous Highland Games of all, the Braemar Gathering, first took place in 1832, later enjoying the patronage of Queen Victoria and future generations of the Royal Family. Many events did not start out as full Highland Games, and the Northern Meeting, first held in Inverness in 1788 and now one of the premier piping contests in Scotland, only added athletic contests a hundred years later. The Argyllshire Gathering, first staged in Oban in 1871, was primarily launched as a meeting for the local aristocracy, with a regatta and grand balls coming before the other contests which locals might still call the Oban Games. It was also in Argyllshire that it was said that Mary Queen of Scots was present at athletic contests at the old castle of Inveraray in 1563, the modern Invereray Games being first staged in 1890. Another Argyllshire event, Taynuilt Games, celebrated its 150th anniversary in 2019.

A typical magazine depiction of 19th Century Highland Games.

From this brief history of Highland Games in Scotland we can conclude that by the end of the 19th century the modern Highland Games meeting made up of heavy events, running and jumping, piping, and Highland dancing had come together as annual events and were very important in the life of their communities. Famous competitors, such as the all-round athlete Donald Dinnie, or pipers such as John McColl, great grand uncle of the famous present piper Angus McColl, became the focus of the Games.

MULL HIGHLAND GAMES: THE CENTENARY

A local community stages its Highland games in the 19th Century.

With the mass emigration of the 19thcentury, Scots settling overseas quickly staged Highland Games on the model of the homeland, with Australia and United States still today holding some of the biggest Games in the world. During both world wars regiments staged their own Highland Games as a diversion from the rigours of war. Spectators have for centuries enjoyed watching runners, jumpers, throwers and hearing the wonderful tones of the pipes on summer days. But, as the poet Norman McCaig tells us, such gatherings have a wider, social purpose:

> They sit on the heather slopes
> and stand six deep round the rope ring.
> Keepers and shepherds in their best plus-fours
> who live mountains apart
> exchange gossip and tall stories.

ERIC MACINTYRE

Highland Games On Mull

As elsewhere in Scotland, informal athletic contests would have taken place on Mull for many centuries as large stones were retrieved from burns and thrown for distance and bragging rights. In common with many other areas, organisation began to emerge in the latter decades of the 19th century and we can read the first reports of these events.

North British Daily Mail - Friday 21st August 1874

The second annual competition in Highland games came off at Tobermory on Wednesday, in a field about a mile from the village. A large crowd of people collected from all parts of Mull, Ardnamurchan and Morvern, and took great interest in the proceedings. Amongst those on the ground we observed Col.Gardyne of Glenforsa; H. Lang and the misses Lang, Glengorm; A. Allan, Esq., of Aros; J. M. M'Kenzie, Esq., of Calgary; J. MacLachlan, Esq., and D. Campbell, Esq., banker's; W. Sprott, Esq., solicitor; Sheriff Ross, &c.

The weather, though threatening in the forenoon, turned out very favourable, which, added to the excellent arrangements of the committee, aided by the active secretary, J. Murray, added much to the success of the meeting.

BOAT RACING

Lugwall Boats of not more than 22 feet keel – 1st Arch. Stewart; 2d, Donald M'Phee.

Four-oared Boats of not more than 20 feet – 1st, Charles M'Lean; 2d, Arch. Master.

Two-oared Boats of not more than 16 feet – C. Thomson, and Arch. M'Master, divided.

MULL HIGHLAND GAMES: THE CENTENARY

Oban Times – Saturday 8th August 1875

TOBERMORY.

Highland Games. - The annual competition in Highland games, &c., was held here on Wednesday. Notwithstanding the very unpropitious weather of the morning the turn-out of spectators and competitors was very large. Messrs Allan, Lang, Ross, and Campbell acted as judges to the entire satisfaction of all interested. Among the visitors present we noted Alexander Allan, Esq.,of Aros, and Mrs Allan; Mr Lang, of Glengorm ;Mr R. Lang ; Sheriff and Mrs Ross ; T. Henderson, Esq., and party, from yacht Selene; Miss Flyter and the Misses Mackenzie ; D. Campbell, Esq., Clydesdale Bank, and Miss Campbell, &c.

The following is the detailed statement of the results:—

GAMES. – Putting Heavy Stone – 1, J. C. Beaton, Bonawe ; 2. D. Campbell, Morvern ; 3, David Grant, Tobermory.

Throwing Heavy Hammer –1, J. C.Beaton, 2, John Smith, Tobermory ; 3, David Grant.

Short Race – 1, Alex. Cameron, Oban ; 2, Alexander Macphail, Aros.

Running Long Leap– 1, John Macphail, Oskamull ; 2, Alexander Cameron ; 3, Charles Macdougall, Tobermory.

Running High Leap – 1, Alexander Macphail ; 2, Alex. Cameron.

Putting Light Stone – 1, D. Campbell ; 2, David Grant ; 3, John Macphail.

Throwing Light Hammer – 1, John Macdougall ; 2,John Smith.

Long Race – 1, J. C. Beaton ; 2, Dugald Macdougall, Oban.

ERIC MACINTYRE

Dancing Highland Fling – 1, Robert Morrison, Salen ;2, Alex. Cameron.

Sword Dance – 1, Robert Morrison ; 2, Alex Cameron.

Tossing the Caber – 1, J. C. Beaton ; 2, John Macdougall, Mull.

Hurdle Race – 1, Alexander Cameron ; 2, JohnMacphail.

Bagpipe Playing – 1, Robert Morrison ; 2,Jas. Macfadyen, Islay.

Sack Race – 1, Alexander Macphail ; 2, Dugald Macdougall ; 3, Donald Macphail, Aros Bridge.

Boys Long Leap – 1, Duncan Fletcher, Glenaros, 15 feet 7 inches ; 2, Donald Macinnes, Tobermory 15 feet 2 inches.

Boys High Leap – 1, Duncan Fletcher, 4 feet ; 2, Alex Lamb, Tobermory, 3 feet 11 inches.

BOAT RACING. - Smacks of 10 Tons and under – 1, Angus Macmillan, Kilchoan ; 2, Archibald Macintyre, Tobermory.

Lugwall Boats – 1, Malcolm Robertson,Tobermory ; 2, Malcolm Macdougall, Tobermory.

Two-oared Race – 1, Charles Maclean, Tobermory ; 2, Don Mackinnon, Tobermory.

Swimming Match, 300 Yards – 1, Angus Macmaster, Tobermory ; 2, Robert Connell, Tobermory.

MULL HIGHLAND GAMES: THE CENTENARY

At the conclusion Mrs Allan, of Aros, gracefully handed over the prizes to the successful competitors. After which three hearty cheers were given for her and for the judges. Much praise is due to the secretary, Mr Murray, who so ably arranged the programme which we may say was carried through without the least hitch. The above meeting has, perhaps, been the most successful yet held, and we have reason to believe that a standing committee is being appointed with the view to making the meeting more interesting and better known than it is at present.

It was not only in Tobermory that Highland Games were staged on Mull. In 1875 Glenforsa Highland Games took place, but competing was confined to residents of Glenforsa and Killiechronan estates, which shows the influence landed proprietors had on the staging of Highland Games on Mull.

In August 1883, Kilninian and Kilmore Highland Games were staged at Dervaig.

In August 1925, the Annual Highland Games were held at Salen, with Colonel Fitzroy Maclean, Chief of Clan Maclean, presiding, along with Brigadier-General Cheape of Tiroran, and Captain Clark of Ulva.

Tiroran Games took place at least until the 1930s.

Willie MacDonald, later minister of Oban Old Parish Church, pole vaulting at Tiroran Games in the 1920s. He broke his leg in those far-off days with no landing pit.

Tiroran Games 1924.

Mull Highland Games

The First World War brought great change to British society. Many women had been left widowed and with dependent children to bring up. There were thousands of wounded ex-servicemen unable to find work, and even among veterans who had not been wounded, the economic situation made it very difficult for them to gain employment. In this climate and to meet some of these immense challenges the Royal British Legion was founded in 1921 with Earl Haig as its first President. It aimed to provide as much help and support as possible to ex-servicemen and war widows and has done so ever since. Local branches were formed to support and care for those in need in their communities.

As with most sporting events, Highland Games had not taken place during the First World War and did not resume until the early 1920s, with some sadly never returning and folding. In Tobermory the local branch of the Royal British Legion saw it as their duty to do everything possible to make life as normal as possible after the horrors of the War. The following paragraphs show its vital role in the foundation of Mull Highland Games.

Meeting of the British Legion on 23rd March 1923

Rev J.M.Menzies presiding.

Inter Alia:

A proposal to have Highland Games was put forward and discussed. It was agreed to put the matter before the next Monthly meeting and in the meantime Mr R. J Brown undertook to write Mr Alastair MacLachlain for use of the field behind Bad- Daraich for practice.

ERIC MACINTYRE

Meeting of British Legion on 4th April 1923

Rev J.M. Menzies presiding.

Inter Alia:- Proposed Highland Games

The proposal to have Highland Games in July brought up at last meeting was again discussed, and the meeting decided to ascertain the feeling of the Town Council on the matter, and if favourable, to invite their cooperation and assistance.

The meeting further resolved to form a committee of those present to make the preliminary arrangements, and the Secretary was asked to send a circular to each person named in the list drawn up, explaining the object and inviting those interested to attend a meeting to be held in the Aros Hall on 15th instant. The Secretary Was also instructed to ascertain the result of Mr Browns application to Mr Alastair MacLachlan for the use of the field behind Bad-Daraich for practice."

Passed and signed Bryce Allan Chairman.

The response from the Town Council was favourable and the first Mull Highland Games were held in July 1923.

We can, therefore, celebrate two major milestones in 2023. First, the 150th anniversary of Highland Games first being staged in Tobermory. Second, the formal establishment of the structure of Mull Highland Games 100 years ago.

MULL HIGHLAND GAMES: THE CENTENARY

Back Row: L. MacLean, A Mackenzie, Charles MacLean, Malcolm MacKay, Duncan Thomas, John Carmichael, Duncan MacQuarrie,

Front Row: R.J. Brown, A.S. MacGilp, William MacLean (Provost), Col Bryce Allan, John M Spink.

The early constitution of the Mull Highland Games Club stated its main aim:

"The object of the Club's existence is to foster Highland Games (as commonly known in the Highlands), and the holding of an Annual Gathering of that description in Tobermory, together with a Concert and Ball on the evening of the Games Day."

For a century, with some minor changes, this aim has remained central to the staging of Mull Highland Games.

Mull Highland Games Club

CONSTITUTION
Laws and By-Laws

Membership Card
(Life or Ordinary)

MCMLIV

The Games Up To The Second World War

As discussed earlier, by the 1920s there was a fairly well established season and circuit of Highland Games events in Scotland. At that time, for example, Luss Games were held the day before Mull Games, Taynuilt the day after, Invereray in mid August and the Argyllshire Gathering in September. It took some time for the now formalised Mull Highland Games to find its place in this summer timetable. This would need competitors to become aware of Tobermory and its Games, and with the establishment of travel arrangements to allow them to take part. This latter aspect was, of course, in the gift of David MacBrayne, the main shipping line operating in the Highlands and Western Isles. The early boats ferrying competitors and spectators to the Mull Highland Games would be the celebrated *Grenadier*, *Fusilier*, and *Loch Fyne*. When that latter vessel came into service in 1931 its Games day voyage from Oban had a pipe band and orchestra aboard. The new steamer attracted favourable comments from passengers and was "so excellently navigated by Captain John Macfarlane and manned by a courteous crew of hardy Highlanders." The only fixed point was that Mull Highland Games would always be held on the third Thursday after the first Monday in July.

The early reports in the Oban Times on the games are quite brief. Mull Highland Games were held at Erray on Thursday 24th July 1924, courtesy of Mr Calder, Erray. The Treasurer was Mr D. Gray, the Secretary Mr L Langton. On 23rd July 1925 Mull Highland Games were staged "in delightful weather, and in presence of 1,500 spectators." In 1926 the Games were staged, "but heavy rain accompanied by a strong wind was a great disappointment," and it was doubted that gate receipts would cover the outgoings. In 1928 the Oban Times reporter wrote that "nothing finer could be wished for than the ideal setting of the Erray grounds, where on the sloping ground which formed a natural grandstand the spectators had an excellent view of every item on the programme." By 1929, the Joint Secretaries were A.M. McKenzie and D. Mitchell, with J.Gray as Treasurer. In 1930 "£100 in prize money" was one of the attractions, as was the "magnificent weather.", with Chas MacLean as Secretary. First prize for open events was 60 shillings or £3 in old money, worth roughly £240 in 2023 equivalence.

Games officials in the early days. From left to right: L.G. Laughton, John B. Yule, Duncan MacQuarrie, Malcolm MacLean, Neil MacKinnon, Robert J. Brown.

In the early staging of the Games most of the competitors would be locals from Mull, Coll, Tiree, or Oban and surrounding areas. One of the best of these would be Robert Allan Maclean who in 1926 set a long jump record of 21ft 4ins which would stand for forty years. He was known as Allan Mann in the manner of Highland nicknames and was the progenitor of a celebrated family dynasty still prominent on Mull to this day. One of his sons, Eoghann, followed his success as an athlete by winning the Chieftain's Cup in 1952.

Left: Eoghann Maclean.

Right: Allan Mann in athletic prime.

MULL HIGHLAND GAMES: THE CENTENARY

Mull has for centuries had a respected piping tradition and in the early years of Mull Highland Games two successful competitors were Duncan Lamont and Ronnie Livingstone.

By the early 1930s Mull Highland Games had taken on more of a structure, and this was in no small measure due to the appointment of Alastair MacIntosh MacLachlainn to succeed T.S. MacMorran as Secretary. This gentleman had been a medical student before the First World War, but joined up in the Scottish Horse and saw action at Gallipoli. He returned to Mull in 1927 to run his small estate at Bad-daraich and bring up his family. He organised the Mull Mod and the Mull Highland Games, where he was always splendidly dressed in straw hat, University Blue blazer, and a kilt. He was clearly a highly efficient Secretary, and placed adverts for the Games months before they were due to be held:

Notification of the forthcoming 1933 Games.

Adverts were placed all over Scotland and those in the Stornoway Gazette were in Gaelic. The Oban Times said after the 1933 Games that "Mr MacLachlainn carried out his exacting secretarial duties in a cool and courteous manner."

Alistair MacLachlainn depicted in a pencil drawing.

His somewhat idiosyncratic approach to matters can be seen in the following postcard which he sent local man, Johnnie Sinclair in 1938:

No emails or text messages in these days!

Alistair MacLachlainn on right, with son Eoghann on left and a relative in the middle.

The 1933 Games welcomed a very special guest as the following cuttings describe in wonderful period language and detail:

Lauder for Tobermory *The Bulletin (Glasgow)*

I hear of an interesting encounter which took place recently between the Provost of Tobermory and Sir Harry Lauder. Quoth the Provost to Sir Harry—"There was a song you used to sing about Tobermory; you'll have made a lot of money out of Tobermory?" The comedian admitted that might be so. "But," queried the Provost, "you'll neffer have seen Tobermory?" "No." "Well, wouldn't it be the nice thing to come and see the beautiful place this summer?"

Goings-On in Mull 27/IV/1933.

The upshot of it all is that Sir Harry Lauder has accepted the invitation to attend Tobermory's Highland Games in July, and will preside at the cailleadh in the evening. So what with a new hotel—that familiar red sandstone landmark above the pier which has been unoccupied for 30 years is to be opened this summer—its first tennis courts, and Sir Harry Lauder, Tobermory is fancying itself no end whateffer.

MULL HIGHLAND GAMES

Oban Times 28/VII/33.

THE COMMITTEE OF THE MULL HIGHLAND Games have not been too fortunate as regards weather for their annual Games during recent years. On Thursday last rain fell heavily during the forenoon, but, to the relief of all concerned, and especially those who had travelled from Oban, Lochgilphead, and other districts, the afternoon was all that could be desired. Hundreds who did not brave the elements in the forenoon found their way to the Erray Grounds overlooking the Sound of Mull.

When the steamer "Lochfyne" (Captain MacFarlane) left Oban North Pier with a very large complement of passengers at 9 a.m., the Mid Argyll Pipe Band (Pipe-Major Greenshields) very appropriately played "The Road to the Isles", and during the journey through the Sound of Mull a Gaelic atmosphere prevailed. Songs from gramophone records by Neil MacLean, Roderick MacLeod and John M. Bannerman were much enjoyed, during which time a passenger was heard inquiring of the captain as to the language in which the music was expressed; the captain's reply being, "That is Gaelic, the first language spoken in the Garden of Eden." "An t-Eilean Muileach" and "Muile na Morbheann" were among the selections so admirably played by the Mid Argyll Band, and as the steamer was entering Tobermory Bay "Tobermory" by Sir Harry Lauder was given on the gramophone, and the passengers joined heartily in the chorus.

While the outward journey took place under depressing weather conditions, the return sail to Oban was much more alluring. A sail through the Sound of Mull on a fine summer evening reveals a quietness and sky effects at sunset which are a joy to witness. Small wonder it is that city dwellers revisit such scenes to find holiday refreshment and reinvigoration in the tangs of loch, clachan and hill.

WELCOME TO SIR HARRY LAUDER.—Sir Harry Lauder, who is to attend the Mull Highland Games on Thursday (to-day), arrived on Monday, 17th July, accompanied by Miss Greta Lauder. On his arrival by the mail boat Lochinvar, Sir Harry was extended a true Highland welcome to the town, which he had made notable in one of his songs, and which fame he has now enhanced by his presence. The popular comedian is staying at the Mishnish Hotel, and the welcome was evidenced by the bunting flown along the main street beyond the pier, and by the eagerness of the crowd who had gathered there. Provost MacLean and Colonel Bryce Allan of Aros extended an official welcome to Sir Harry on behalf of the town.

Harry Lauder's signature in the Mishnish Guest book.

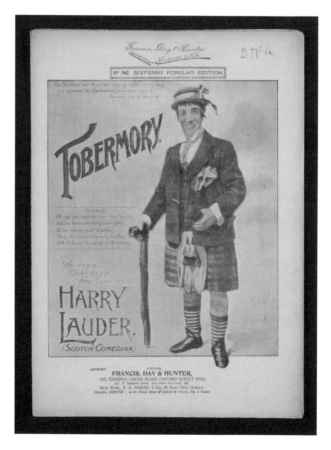

(No reports exist that Sir Harry entertained the audience at the concert with his famous *Tobermory* song!)

By the time of this much publicised event, Tobermory Games was attracting the very best competitors in piping, dancing, and heavy and light athletics. One of the most famous was the legendary George Clark who competed in the heavy events at Tobermory from the early 1930s to the early 1960s, a truly remarkable career span. His 1930s rivals included Edward Anderson and A.J. Stuart. A 1937 report spoke of the tourists on the trip to the Games being "heard remarking on the excellent physique and manly bearing of the athletic champions, many of whom had travelled long distances to compete."

George Clark tossing the caber at Tobermory in the 1930s.

In piping the famous MacPherson family members graced the boards along with Pipe Major John MacDonald, Hugh Kennedy, and Duncan Lamont from Pennycross.In dancing the honours went to R.M. Cutherbertson, J.L. Mackenzie, Molly Adams and Mary Aitken. In the running and jumping events the brothers Edward and George Masson took many prizes and records in stiff competition with the dual Powderhall Sprint winner Willie MacFarlane, Jim Black, Angus Macintyre, Dan Clark, Neil MacArthur and Powderhall middle distance champions Nell MacCallum and Duncan Macintyre.

When Sir Harry Lauder and his niece visited in 1933 they stayed at the Mishnish Hotel whose proprietors were Duncan and Anne MacLeod. Their son Bobby, of whom more later, won the chanter competition in 1933, and in 1935 his sister Ishbel won the local schools Highland Fling event.

Bobby MacLeod, Hugh Kain, Ishbel MacLeod, Bella Kain, Miss Gough, Sine Campbell, Unknown. Miss Gough taught Highland dancing.

Bobby MacLeod, Hugh Kain, Ishbel MacLeod, Bella Kain, Miss Gough,
Sine Campbell. Miss Gough taught Highland Dancing.

Medal won by Ishbel Macleod in 1935, designed by the multi-talented Alistair
MacLachlainn.

MULL HIGHLAND GAMES: THE CENTENARY

Within ten years of its foundation in 1923, Mull Highland Games had a well organised committee and stewarding structure. A 1937 picture shows this fine body of people.

The top picture is of the Games Committee in 1937. The bottom one is of the names (not in order) on the back of the photo in the Mull Museum. While some members are known the author did not wish to make wrong assumptions.

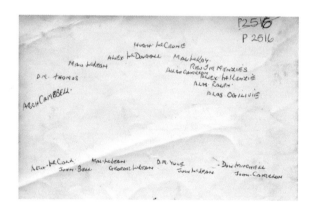

In 1937, the first year when Sir Charles MacLean was Hereditary Chieftain, the South of Mull Pipe Band under Pipe Major William Gordon led the parade. The Torosay Castle party included the famous English actress (Dame) Irene Vanbrugh and the 1938 event was the "Best day in years..." In 1938 the Tobermory Nursing Association took on the catering arrangements for the Games and raised £30 for its funds. In 1939 a "Record attendance in glorious weather" was reported. Among the spectators was Prince Henry of Bavaria. A train derailment meant that the *King George* was an hour late arriving for the Games, forcing the committee into swift action to ensure the programme caught up time before the boats left the pier for the return journeys.

Prince Henry of Bavaria, third left front row, watches the events.

In 1944 David MacBrayne Ltd funded the production of a series of films under the title of "Isles of Youth." They were intended to show the beauty of the Western Isles, presumably as a way of attracting tourists who would use MacBrayne's boats to travel. The third film has some footage of Mull Highland Games from an undated year in the late 1930s. It can be viewed online and may be the only extant film of that pre-war games era.

The Games In The 1940s And 1950s

In common with all Highland Games in Scotland, Mull saw no Games during the Second World War. Some did not return when peace came and, for example, Inveraray Games were not staged again until 1958. But Mull Highland Games had established itself so successfully in the 1930s that it was financially sound enough to be held again in 1948. A record attendance of 3000 was recorded, with many American and French visitors in the crowd. In 1949, Major Duncan McCallum MP for Argyll, dashed from London to be taken on a small boat to Grasspoint on Mull to attend the Games Concert, an event for which so many turned up that some had to be turned away in disappointment.

There were several important changes in the running of the Games by this time. Alastair MacLachlainn had completed his medical studies and after service in the Second World War went off to South Georgia as medical officer on a whaling ship. The Games also by now had a Hereditary Chieftain whose family would remain in that role to this day. Sir Charles Hector Fitzroy MacLean, Bart., of Duart and Morvern later, Lord Maclean, Lord Chamberlain to Queen Elizabeth II. Sir Charles had succeeded to the title and Chief of Clan MacLean on the death of his grandfather in 1936. His own father, Major Hector Fitzroy Maclean, had been briefly Chieftain of Mull Highland Games before his death in 1932. He had been succeeded for a few years as Chieftain

by Captain Charles L. MacLean R.N. of Ballinluig. Sir Charles had served in the Second World War and afterwards returned to Mull, to the ancestral Maclean seat of Duart Castle, to look after his heritage. He became Chief Scout of the Commonwealth and although a very busy man, always tried to be in attendance for Mull Games to lead the parade to the field, present trophies and attend the Games Concert in the evening, ably supported by Lady Maclean and his children.

Sir Charles Maclean as Chief Scout.
(Painting by John Wyndham Hughes-Hallett)

Sir Charles MacLean leading the parade around 1950,with the Glasgow Police Pipe Band.

The 1948 Heavy Events officials. Back left, Hector Macgregor, Neil Maclean (Derryguaig), John MacDonald, Alex MacDougall, Hugh Gillies. Front (left) athletes George Clark and right Jack Hunter.

J L MacKenzie, Aberdeen, A F Forbes, Glasgow, and Jack MacConochie, Ruislip, compete in the Sword Dance.

ERIC MACINTYRE

Pictures of the Games field in 1950.

Mull Games July 1959

Provost Charles MacLean, the chairman of the Games, chats with Mr Angus MacIntyre, the recently appointed honorary treasurer, himself a former noted athlete.

If one can apply the much over-used word "legend" to a ship, then RMS *King George V* is worthy of that accolade for its role in the history of Mull Highland Games. Since

the mid 1930s it had plied its daily summer voyages from Oban to Iona and Staffa via Tobermory on both the outward and return journeys. Leaving Oban at 9am on Games Day, as that fine man and MacBrayne's employee, Jimmy Henderson, would report to the Games Secretary: "Full to the gunnels" with spectators and competitors. The *King George* had also rescued troops from Dunkirk in 1940. Brigadier John Macfarlane recalls vividly the eager anticipation of its approach to Tobermory on Games Day.

"Sharp eyes were kept out for the sight of the King George V racing up the Sound beyond Calve island. Before it came alongside at MacBraynes Pier half of Tobermory seem to congregate on the upper balcony of the Pier building to spot friends, relatives, and regular visitors and athletes attending the Games."

The Claymore at the Tobermory pier on Games day in the 1950s.

Apart from the *King George* from Oban, other ships, including the *Lochearn*, *Claymore*, and *Lochnevis* would come in from Coll, Tiree, Mingary and Lochaline to swell the numbers at the Games. Alistair MacNeill first arrived from Tiree in 1953 to run in a boys' relay race against locals Gordon Grant, Pete Mason, and Robin Cowe. As the boat approached the pier, an escapologist was being tied in chains before being put in a locked canvas bag, watched over by a local policeman. As one wag observed: "By Jove, they are tough on law breakers in Tobermory!"

These steamers all called at Tobermory in the years before the Oban to Craignure ferry began in 1964. As Angus Macintyre, observed:

> "Och, the traffic that was flowin'
> Of Bodachs and their Dames,
> And effery one was goin'
> To Tobermory Games."

An Exile's Perspective

The Island of Mull, like all on the West Coast, has seen many of its natives become part of the Great Highland diasporato all parts of the world. But memories of "home" and the Mull Games remain strong. Anna Eifert (nee Bowman) has lived in America for over forty years but remembers attending when young.

"My memories of the time are mainly from early childhood when I was aged 5-12, and we were living at Killiechronan. My mother and father used to pile all of us "wee ones," as they called us, into the back of dad's old Black Riley, I believe, and off we would go on a big adventure to Tobermory! Our lives were largely at that time, the farm and Gruline school, so it was exciting to see other parts of the island. I mostly remember walking

up the steep road to the games field. As you approached, the sound of the announcers and the bagpipes playing, and as you arrived, seeing the field opening up to a tableau of beautiful colours and busy competitions going on. We as children were quite awed by this sight. Both my mother and usually my older sister, somehow, would shepherd us up to the hill to select a good spot for us all to watch the day's events. I remember a rucksack of sandwiches, fruit, and biscuits for snacks. I'm sure my mum didn't relish navigating the tea tent with all those children! We always had a blanket to sit on and were usually cold. I remember because our mother had us all dressed in our Sunday best for such a special occasion. My sisters and I loved the highland dancing, especially the younger children. The boys, of course, were more interested in the hammer, caber, and field competitions.

As I got older, about 14 years old, I was allowed to go to the Games dance in the Aros Hall. That event was always such a happy occasion for me. I loved to watch the adults dancing the Quadrilles and the Eightsome Reel, among many other dances. The music was wonderful, and it still brings a tear to my eye just thinking about it. Those were happy days!"

A New Secretariat

When Alistair MacLachlainn relinquished his role as Secretary, the task was taken up jointly by Hugh Kain and John Cameron. As we have seen, Hugh had won prizes for dancing at the Games in the 1930s and John had been on the Committee since the 1930s. The role was both onerous and complex, involving such tasks as liaising with the Golf Club over the use of Erray Park; advertising and publicising the Games; liaising with MacBraynes over shipping; booking the tents from Blacks of Greenock; processing the entries and the printed programme; organising the Concert and Games Dance; and numerous other small, but time-consuming, matters. John was colloquially known as *Balachan*, Gaelic for boy, and Hugh was manager in the Post Office.

The essential duo of Hugh Kain(left) and John Cameron on Games Day in the 1950s.

ERIC MACINTYRE

John Macfarlane writes: *When I was a bit older, I became an assistant to the two big characters who organised the games. "Balachan" Cameron and Hugh Kain, who, in typical Tobermory humour, particularly during the Cold War, were known as B&K. They were highly organised and oversaw the whole operation from the set-up to the wonderful Games Concert and to the last dance on the Games Night Dance.*

Brigadier John Macfarlane.

Hugh Kain left Mull for work in 1959 and although no longer joint Secretary, came back every year on his annual holidays to play a major part as he had always done. The continuity of his family in the Games to this day will be covered later. John Cameron remained Secretary until his death in 1968. His successor as Secretary, Lorn Macintyre, described John as "the great impresario, the Lew Grade of Tobermory." Balachan was very proud of a riposte he once made to criticism. An old timer, whom we shall call Alan, met John on the games field as final preparations were being made for the big day to follow. Alan said: "Ah Balachan, turning up when all the wok has been done." John reached in his breast pocket for his Parker and retorted: "Alan, the pen is mightier than the caber."

Iain MacFadyen in 2023 with the chanter he won aged twelve.

In the late 1940s and 1950s the quality of competitors at Mull Highland Games was of the highest calibre. In piping, sixteen-year-old John D. Burgess won his first trophy at Tobermory in 1950, the same year that he won the gold medals at both Oban and Inverness. The MacFadyen brothers, John and Iain, had Mull ancestors and Iain won a chanter at the games as a twelve year old. Their uncle, Allan Beaton, was later piping convenor at the Games. Pipe Major Ronald Lawrie always had a busy day at the Games from marching to the field leading the Glasgow Police Band to competing and winning the highest level competitions. Other leading competitors of that

40

time were Ronnie MacCallum, John McLellan and Hector MacFadyen. In 1958 a total of 28 pipers took part in the open competitions.

The Games committee in the 1950s. From left: Duncan MacQuarrie, Alistair MacLachlainn, Donnie Yule, Hughie Gillies, John MacDonald, Archie Cattanach, Hugh Kain, Allan Cameron, Co.Charles MacLean, John Cameron, Archie MacMaster, John Gunn, Bill Heath, Jack Bushell.

Pipe Major John D. Burgess. Picture courtesy Robert Wallace and Piping Press.

John and Iain MacFadyen (Piping Press).

Pipe Major Ronald Lawrie in his Glasgow Police uniform (Piping Press).

Ronald Lawrie and Iain Macfadyen would later serve "on the bench" as piping judges at Mull Highland Games.

In the heavy events George Clark continued to be successful into his fourth decade of competing. His main rivals were Henry Gray, Sandy Sutherland, and Jay Scott. In 1959 a young Bill Anderson had the first year of what would be a sterling career on the Highland Games circuit.

In dancing the leading performers included Betty Jessiman, Catriona Buchanan, Billy Forsyth, and Sheena MacDonald. A young Jean Swanston first danced at Tobermory in 1959 and would go on to great success over the next two decades.

Sylvia Henderson and Jean Swanston at Mull Games in 1959.

Jean recalls these wonderful times: "I was probably 11 when I started competing at Tobermory. My Dad worked on the railways, so we travelled everywhere by train. He had maybe 9 free passes every year as well as 'privileged tickets' which included the ferries, ideal for a trip to Tobermory. Coming from Luss on the Wednesday Mum, Dad and I would get back to Glasgow and get the night train up to Oban.

We arrived in the early hours of the morning and were allowed to remain on the train until it was time for the 9am boat. My Dad used to go out to a bakery and come back to the train with freshly baked hot rolls and fizzy lemonade. That put me off fizzy drinks for life.

The 2-hour sail on the *King George V* to Tobermory was magical for me. I loved to be outside for the entire journey and be totally windswept. One year, wrestlers had slept in their van on the pier and almost missed the sailing. I remember one of them pole vaulting onto the boat as it was moving!

When we arrived at Tobermory there was always a competitors' bus which took us halfway up the hill and then we walked the rest of the short distance to the Games field. Toilets were at the very top of the hill, usually a hessian cloth round a couple of seats which had the seat insert missing. There was a year when the ladies' powder room as they called it had not been erected. The announcer told the crowd that ladies should use the gents, and the gents were to jump the wall!

In my memory, all the competitors who travelled to Mull were at the top of their game. Dancing was no different. I remember asking Betty Jessiman if she was going to the "North" Games. Now Betty stayed in Huntly and I stayed in Edinburgh, so her answer to me was, no, she was going to the "West" Games.

Quite often it was windy on the dancing board, but I always enjoyed doing a step called the reverse points in the Sword Dance. Billy Forsyth dancing in the next set on the board, and said because I did that step, he thought the wind must be ok, but it wasn't when he did the same step.

And there was only one year when the weather was so bad that the dancing had to be taken into a small hall further down the hill. Normally sawdust on the board would see us manage to keep dancing outside, but this was monsoon style rain. My Dad bought waterproof clothing in the ships' chandlers as it was so bad, and Mum and I nearly walked past him as we didn't recognise him.

One year dancer Charlie Mill, who was always good fun at the board, had arrived at the Games and forgotten his tartan trews for under his kilt. I suggested he ask Iain C. Macdonald who was piping for the dancing. Right there and then in the middle of the field, Iain C. took them off and handed them over to Charlie, who made a joke about there being a split in the pants, so he didn't know which way to wear them.

My husband John was an athlete and remembers a funny incident concerning a local worthy in the mile race one year, when his teeth fell out during the race. He just collected them from the trackside once the race was over.

Now the boat home was always great fun. The Glasgow Police Pipe Band complete with bass drummer who was somewhat unsteady on his feet, played for an Eightsome Reel one time and we dancers danced on the top deck. This was not an easy task with the wind, the sea swell, and pipers getting faster. There was always music and laughter. John and I would have a meal with the heavies, and a famous Englishman wanted the seat beside him left empty. He ordered a meal for himself and a meal for his invisible friend who was "at the toilet"… and promptly ate both meals.

I must have enjoyed the Tobermory experience as I was still competing there after our 2 sons were born 10 years apart. On more than one occasion, when the boys were small, we made a bed for one of them on the field whether it was rain or shine. Congratulations Mull, on your centenary!"

Jean Swanston dancing at Braemar Games. Her husband John Robertson is on her left, shielding his eyes from the sun while admiring his wife's vigorous performance of the Irish Washerwoman.

In the running and jumping events many local competitors such as Duncan MacIver and Norman MacGilp held up Mull's reputation against the open competitors. The most successful of these was Gordon Grant from Iona, whose range of events extended from the 100 yards, up to the mile and included the long jump and hop, step, and jump. Gordon won the Chieftain's Cup in 1956. He recalls one year when he slipped on the wet turf of the tight bends at Erray Park and badly spiked himself. He was taken to the Mishnish Hotel and tended to by Dr Bill Lloyd, husband of the dancer Ishbel mentioned earlier and brother-in-law of Bobby MacLeod. Assessing the wound Dr.Lloyd told Gordon "I don't know whether to stitch it or give you a dram and send you on your way!"

Left: Dr Bill Lloyd. Right: Gordon Grant in 2023 with the Chieftain's Cup he won in 1956.

Gordon Grant and Alistair MacNeill in 1961 with well earned silverware.

A fellow competitor of Gordon's was Fergie MacDonald from Acharacle, later to go on to world renown as The Ceilidh King of accordion music. Fergie competed in the sprints and jumps events and one year tied for the points necessary to win the Chieftain's Cup. However, it was decided that the tie-breaker event should be the sack race, and Fergie lost out to another local competitor. Gordon Grant never forgot this seeming injustice and many years later while visiting Fergie, he gave him his own replica of the Chieftain's Cup, a sporting gesture which Fergie remembers as being in the true spirit of Highland Games. On his first visit to the Games Fergie stayed on for the dance in the Aros Hall. Having booked no accommodation, he chose instead to sleep under the stars near to the famous "God is Love" inscription on the rocks. Next morning, he boarded the Lochbuie and had a successful day at the Kilchoan Regatta and Sports.

Fergie in 2023 with the cup given to him by Gordon Grant.

Many excellent light athletes competed in the 1950s, including Andy Mitchell, later starter and handicapper at the games, W Finlay, Billy MacPherson and Jay Scott. Jay was an amazing athlete with an all-round range never seen before or since in the Highland Games or arguably not even in amateur athletics in Scotland. Hailing from Inchmurrin Island in Loch Lomond, Jay and his brother Tom toured the Highland games circuit all over Scotland. Jay was fast enough to finish fourth in the famous Powderhall New Year Sprint, he was capable of long jumping over 22ft and doing 47ft in the hop, step and jump, brave enough to pole vault over 11ft with no landing bed and springy enough to high jump 6ft 3.5ins at Tobermory in 1956. This record still stands and can lay claim to being one of the oldest standing records on the Highland games circuit. Bill MacCallum remembers this jump vividly: "My first memory was 1955 when I was 2 months short of my 8th birthday. Looking back now 68 years later I appreciate I witnessed a very special event which has not been bettered in all these years. My memory is vague but I can recall the high jump event in which the great all-round athlete Jay Scott from Inchmurrin on Loch Lomond won against a top jumper from the USA. My view was restricted by the crowd and my parents allowed me to go to the top of the banking where, standing under a flagpole, I watched Jay Scott clear 6ft 3.5inches. This was an amazing jump considering Jay used a scissors technique and did not have the luxury of landing on soft crash mats."

If that were not enough Jay could do all the heavy events and was the overall Scottish Heavy Events Champion in 1958.At a Highland Games Jay would flit between the heavy and light events, taking off his kilt to compete in the high jump, always, of course, being careful that he had his shorts on first! He was handsome and possessed a charismatic personality. Many thought wrongly that he was the athlete depicted on the Scott's Porridge Oats box, and his athletic career was very like Geordie of the famous 1950s film of that title. Fergie Macdonald was once hitching a lift to Arisaig Games when Jay came along in his van and picked him up. With a steel vaulting pole on the roof and despite driving very fast, they were late arriving at the Games. The high jump had just finished and although Jay pleaded to be allowed a jump, the judges refused. Like a Hollywood hero Jay cleared what had been the winning height in his kilt and brogues, but the judges would not budge on the prizes!

Jay Scott high jumping.

Another story about this remarkable athlete took place at Tobermory pier. Arriving back late from the Games Field, Jay, to the Captain's consternation, simply planted his vaulting pole and sprang on to the deck of the *King George*! No film exists of this daring method of boarding and even if a bit exaggerated, it still feels so typical of this truly wonderful athlete.

Jay Scott clearing over 11ft in the pole vault at Tobermory.

ERIC MACINTYRE

MULL HIGHLAND GAMES AT TOBERMORY.
Final spurt in the 100 Yards Race by such well-known
runners as :- Jay Scott, Andrew Mitchell, W. Findlay, W. MacPherson.
etc. etc.

Jay Scott putting the shot.

MULL HIGHLAND GAMES: THE CENTENARY

In 1958, Sir Charles Maclean dramatically demonstrated his great commitment to Mull Highland Games. He had to be in London on business on the day before the event and caught the sleeper train north. He alighted at Crianlarich and took a car to Oban in time to board the *King George* for a more leisurely trip to Tobermory, in time to lead the parade and join an estimated 3500 spectators at Erray Park. In 1959 the Chieftain had to be in India on Scouting duties and did not attempt a swift return to Mull! Colonel Charles Maclean ably deputised as Chieftain in his absence.

The 1958 parade with Colonel Charles Maclean, left, in charge with his Chieftain beside him.

In 1959 Angus Macintyre was appointed manager of the Clydesdale Bank in Tobermory. A former competitor at Tobermory in the 1930s, he took up the role of Treasurer of Mull Games.

The Games In The 1960s And 1970s

In November 1959 a committee meeting of the Mull Highland Games Club discussed the importance of trying to build up a contingency fund as a financial buffer against unexpected problems and expenses. Up to this time the main sources of income were gate receipts on the day itself or donations by individuals known as Patrons. The Club had always been active in putting on other events such as the annual Spring Concert, jumble sales, the very popular Forty Club functions in the Western Hotel, the annual Fancy Dress event in the Aros Hall and a dance at Christmas time, also in the Aros Hall. These events were very important in the annual social calendar of Tobermory and Mull in general at a time when it should be noted that television was in its infancy in the Highlands and even those lucky enough to have a set had reception that looked like bullets crossing the screen! In 1960 the Christmas Dance included a regional heat of the Miss Scotland contest.

Aros Hall Dancing, The Games Christmas Dance

MULL HIGHLAND GAMES: THE CENTENARY

That 1959 meeting decided to add yet another event to the Club's busy schedule. Approval was given for an inaugural Burns Supper to be held, and with the ever willing and efficient help of the proprietor Donald MacLean and his wife Greta, the first Supper took place in January 1960 in the Western Isles Hotel. Although these events were well attended and much appreciated locally, they were never intended to massively swell the Club's coffers. The amount required annually for prizes on the day and all other expenses made finance a constant worry for a voluntary organisation.

```
                    TOAST  LIST
            _____

            Chairman, Angus Macintyre, Esq.

"The Queen" ..................... Dr. R. Fawcitt
"Our Patrons" .......... Provost A. R. C. MacLeod
Reply ................ J. A. L. Forrester, Esq.

              I N T E R V A L

"The Isle of Mull" ....... The Secretary of State
                                    for Scotland.
        The Rt. Hon. Michael Noble. M.P.
Reply ... Sir Chas. H.F. MacLean of Duart. Bart.

              I N T E R V A L

   "Wi' merry sangs and friendly cracks,
        I wat ye dinna weary."

"The Immortal Memory" ...... Angus Macintyre, Esq
"The Secretary of State" ...... Col. A. G. Miller
"The Lassies" ........J. G. Mathieson, Esq.
              Convener. Argyll County Council
Reply ... Mrs. A. E. Cameron of the "Oban Times"

              I N T E R V A L

"The Host and Hostess" .... Lady MacLean of Duart
"The Chairman" ..... A. H. Allan, Esq. of Linndhu
Vote of thanks to Artistes, etc. ..... The Chair

          "Auld  Lang  Syne"

      A "TIT BIT" BEFORE YOU LEAVE
```

Some well kent names!

The risks discussed at the 1959 meeting soon came into sharp focus for the Club. In 1960, a national seaman's strike was in the offing as Games Day approached. Displaying brinkmanship worthy of the later Cuban crisis, the Committee held off cancelling and the strike was called off two days before the Games, going ahead without a major hit to finances. However, as we all know, the weather in the Western Isles is a chameleon of the first order, with dreamy sunsets and stunning views quickly replaced by gales and driving rain. Such was the case in 1962 when a freak summer storm wreaked havoc on Erray Park, keeping the spectators away. The MacBraynes steamers only brought 650 to the Games as opposed to 1800 the previous year. The Chieftain, ever eager to attend in spite of a busy schedule, had planned to be there in the morning and leave after lunch to get a launch to Oban from Grasspoint. However, he was forced to abandon this plan and leave by the morning steamer. Instead. In his absence, A.H. Allan of Aros led the parade and welcomed the Moderator of the Church of Scotland, Dr Nevile Davidson to the Games. However, even that esteemed cleric had no influence over the weather. The rains were unrelenting and Katriona Lloyd remembers her mother having to go to Brown's to get a second oilskin for Dr Bill Lloyd, official starter on that day. The tents blew down and the Highland Dancing had to be transferred indoor to the Drill Hall. Rhoda, daughter of Bobby MacLeod, remembers how exciting this was for her as a young child as she watched the dancers on the shoulders of her Grannie Anne.

The 1962 storm braved only by the hardy.

The major blow to income could have proved terminal, but Angus Macintyre both Treasurer and local bank manager, managed to "finesse" the accounts and so keep the Games going for another day.

Memories Of Games Week

Looking back, all readers will have memories of the week leading up to the day itself. John Macfarlane writes:

"Excitement started to grow during the previous week, when the men of the village started to prepare the field, putting up, marquees, marking the running tracks and setting up the platforms for dancing and piping. One of the highlights was the presence of two of Lucille Cameron's sons, big Al and Iain, who were Metropolitan policeman and enormous guys. After the evening's work was done, and 'refreshments' were produced, they used to take part in a competition called the *Maide Leisg*, where two men sat 2 to 2, with a strong axeshaft placed between their toes, which they both gripped, and then pulled. One of them either was pulled up or went sideways. Needless to say, the Ohio Camerons always won hands down. We boys enjoyed the whole thing enormously and got in the way of everyone while we were 'helping. "

Maide Leisg or Lazy Stick being hard fought in the 1950s. A young Robert MacLeod on the right.

The wrestlers do battle.

55

Katie MacDougall and Meareag Kennedy selling programmes in the 1950s.

John Macfarlane continues: "After the *King George* and other ships had disgorged their passengers on Games Day the parade made its way up to Erray Park. The Glasgow Police Pipe Band formed up at the Coalree, just behind the pier. They all seemed to be six footers and when they put on their busbies they seemed to be giants to me They paraded along the front Street as far as the Town Clock, followed by a raggle-taggle crowd, including me! The parade, then wound back up the Back Brae, past the Western Isles Hotel and so on to the Games Field - a long march for the pipers."

The events then took place in one of the most wonderful amphitheatres in Scotland for the staging of a Highland Games. The Patrons and distinguished guests were permitted to sit on former church pews near the finishing line for the races. When the events at Erray Park were over the crowd would make its way back down the hill, either to the main street or to the pier to board a boat for home. Friends would be bade farewell until the next time, and if the clock permitted, this would be preceded by a dram in the Mishnish where pipers would attempt to play after perhaps one too many.

The MacBraynes ships would head for Coll, Tiree, Mingary, Lochaline and Oban. These journeys would be made in good spirits in all meanings of that word. On the *King George*, Jean Swanston remembers eightsome reels to the music of "mortal

Glasgow police pipers" and below deck the bar would do a roaring trade. On the journey back to Coll and Tiree Alistair MacNeill remembers folk in "good trim", as Para Handy would say. "It would be a non-stop ceilidh, but unfortunately, we were too young to be involved in such "après games" activities."

Bill Anderson had to be cautious in his post Games celebrations as he had to drive straight from Oban to Inverness and on to Dunbeath Games next day.

People from Coll, returning home from Games Day.

The Games Concert And Dance

When the visitors had left, the natives took a breather or more likely, another drop of nectar. Games day was far from over. The Concert would commence around 7.30 pm with the Chieftain or Col. Charles Maclean welcoming all before Angus Macintyre took over as compere. John Macfarlane writes: "The Concert was always a great occasion, with many fine singers and musicians, notable among them the tenor Kenny Macrae whom I recall always sang 'Maid of Morvern' to the holder of the title, the daughter of Maclean of Duart and Morvern. It must have been a source of embarrassment to the poor young girl sitting in the front row of a packed Aros Hall! The Concert always opened with the entire audience singing the first verse of our Island Anthem, 'An t-Eilean Muileach' (The Isle of Mull) and it is a measure of the number present who were Gaelic speakers that the rafters of the Hall rang to the emotion of the occasion, and the strong and beautiful Gaelic of the song. Piper Angus Morrison had played all day for the dancers at Erray Park, but was still on hand to get the event off to a rousing start. The sisters Helen T and May Margaret Macmillan sang Gaelic songs, Pibroch MacKenzie charmed on the fiddle and many visiting artists gave of their best."

Eventually even Angus Macintyre and Balachan could not find the energy for a whole day and evening of duties, so the Concert was moved to the Friday night. Games Day in Tobermory had begun before the *King George* docked, but even after the concert the day was not over. John Macfarlane concludes his reminiscences: "After the concert, the hall was cleared of people to allow the seats to be moved to have a good space for dancing and for sitting out. The floor would be duly sprinkled with "Sliipperene" to allow feet to glide more easily over the wooden floor. In the interval while the hall was being cleared for the dance to begin, many of the Young Bloods were exchanging sips out of half bottles of whisky in the rather malodorous gents' toilet, which stood at the back of the Aros Hall, a fact that meant that by the time they got upstairs, they were raring to go! Except obviously, for couples, the dancers split up on gender lines with the girls sitting along one side of the room and the men, either standing in a feckless rather shy bunch at the top of the back stairs, leading to the hall or standing on the opposite side to the girls, ready to rush across to their chosen partner, as soon as the dance was announced.

The music was provided by the peerless Bobby Macleod, Callum MacLean or a visiting band. Tobermory boys and girls prided themselves on being good dancers (which we all were) and the night developed fast and furious, with the temperature rising in the hall with all these energetic bodies.

MULL HIGHLAND GAMES: THE CENTENARY

Hugh Kain seemed to have appointed himself as a keeper of the peace, and drifted about rather menacingly, wearing a pair of dark leather dancing pumps. He was reputed to be an expert on jujitsu, and certainly any miscreants got short shrift and were arm-locked down the stairs, and out of the hall in very short order! As I remember it, the Dance attracted people from all over the north of the island, and I can certainly recall farmers coming from Arle (my father called them Les Arlesiens) who appeared in suits, wearing white gloves, so as not to stain in the dresses of the ladies with their work-worn hands. I can still see them in the middle of reel sets, with their gloved hands facing outward on their hips as they pas de basqued round facing their partners. A touch of a bygone Mull! Alas, all good things come to an end and with the approaching dawn, there was the usual scramble for the last waltz, where the boys made a beeline for the lady of their choice, who had given permission to walk them home! But not quite yet! When I was young, I think it became a tradition that Bobby MacLeod, an excellent Piper, shouldered and tuned his bagpipes and we all marched along the main street behind the Piper to dance a final reel on MacBrayne's Pier where it had all started with the arrival of the *King George* on the previous morning!"[NB in the archives of Mull Highland Games no Risk Assessments have been found for these pier reels!] And then, as John Macfarlane recalls fondly, "it was home in the cool of the dawn with the rising sun making pools of light on Tobermory Bay."

When Bobby MacLeod died at the tragically early age of 65 in January 1991, BBC Scotland broadcast a memorial programme hosted by Bobby's friend Robbie Shepherd, with contributions by band leaders who were Bobby's friends and admirers. Ian Powrie had a wonderful memory of what must have been the most melodious Games Dance ever. "It was in the middle 1950s, I imagine," Ian recollected. "Bobby rang me up and said: I've let all the band go on holiday and I've to play at the Games Dance. It's going to be dodgy, playing on my own. Will you come up [to Tobermory] and give me a hand? I'll ring Jimmy [Shand] and if he comes, will you come? I got a phone call from Jimmy. He said: Are you going? I said: Aye, we'll go up and have a tune. It was marvellous, of course, but on the road up, the tickle, the laugh was, Jimmy's car was scattered with pipe books. Jimmy says to me: I play all they tunes, ye ken, son, but I'll no' likely play them the same as he [Bobby] plays them. We're sitting thumbing through pipebooks all the way up to Tobermory... We sat down at the dance and had a tune. There was Jimmy, Bobby, and Willie Lowe [from Tobermory] on the piano, Dickie McGill on the drums, and myself with the fiddle. It was a lovely tune. I enjoyed it fine."

Left to right: Fenwick MacDougall, Davy Whitehead, Willie Lowe, Bobby Macleod, Billy Ford, "Pibroch" MacKenzie. "I would say that Bobby was really a piper who played an accordion," according to John D. Burgess, superlative piper, friend, admirer of Bobby.

Bobby MacLeod recorded two marvellous sets of tunes "To the Games" and "After the Games" which readers are advised to listen to with a glass in hand.

After the revels of Games day the hardy would have to return to Erray Park the next day to return their fairway to the golf club, now peppered with a few holes from hammer throws.

Callum Maclean band with Alistair ("Scent") Mackenzie and Davy MacAllister.

Many other bands have played for the Games Dance and these include:

The Legionnaires; Tobermory String Band; Salen Band, Andrew Rankine; Heather Broadcasting Band; Ian Nicholson Band; The Sloop, Jim Johnstone, Jim MacLeod, Skipinnish, West Telferton Band, Neil McKechran, John Renton, Iain MacPhail, Alan Gardner, Allan McIntosh.

Similarly, Games Day has always been graced by a pipe band and these have included: Glasgow Police Pipe Band; Mid Argyll Pipe Band; South Mull Pipe Band; Glasgow Police; Ceannloch Pipe Band; Oban Pipe Band; Isle of Tiree Pipe Band; Mull and Iona Pipe Band;8th Argylls; The Highlanders; Oban High School Pipe Band.

Mull Highland Games has always seen big characters, whether as competitors or officials. Of the latter none came bigger than Allan Cameron, known affectionately as "Big Al". A former policeman, Al always ensured that he was in Tobermory for Gamesweek and helped to erect the Blacks of Greenock's hired tents. Big Al wielded the sledgehammer to put up the posts to rope off the arena and dug the primitive latrines of those days. As a former heavy athlete and Chieftain's Cup winner, he knew the little ways of athletes and acted as an empathetic official on Games Day.

Big Al in typical pose on Games Day.

Another character from this era was Bobby Maclean, known affectionately as "Bobby Butter". Working as a member of the County roads repair crew, Bobby would take his

Bobby as we will always remember him.

annual holidays at Glasgow Fair time and "donate" much of it to Mull Highland Games. Often walking from his Drumfin home, he would arrive on Monday ready to help set out the field. Going home only to swim his sheep to Calve Island, he would help put up the tents, aid Big Al in latrine digging, but above all, keep his fellow volunteers amused with great stories and the driest sense of humour. On Games Day he was to be found helping at the heavy events and his week of vacation ended on Friday helping clear the field. In the 100 years of the history of Mull Highland Games it would be hard to think of a more dedicated person who did so much and asked nothing in return. On his death Robert MacLeod wrote of him as "Bobby Maclean, gentle man."

List of Previous Cup Winners

Chieftain's Cup

1930	Livingstone, L.
1931	MacCallum, D.
1932	Black, Jas.
1933	Stewart, A.
1934	McCallum, I. D.
1935	MacArthur, N. N.
1936	MacLean, R. N.
1937	Lamont, B.
1938	MacInnes, J. G.
1939	MacDonald, D.
1948	MacColl, Iain
1949	Stewart, J.
1950	MacLean, H.
1951	Cameron, A.
1952	MacDonald, J.
1953	MacFadyen, L.
1954	MacDonald, C.
1955	MacRae, F.
1956	Grant, G.
1957	Ferguson, F.
1958	Lamont, H.
1959	Bell, C.
1960	MacLean, Ronnie

Brown Cup

1936	Lamont, D.
1937	Lamont, D.
1938	MacFadyen, H.
1939	MacFadyen, H.
1948	Lamont, D.
1949	Lamont, D.
1950	Lamont, D.
1951	Campbell, A.
1952	Campbell, A.
1953	MacFadyen, H.
1954	MacFadyen, H.
1955	MacFadyen, D.
1956	MacFadyen, H.
1957	MacFadyen, H.
1958	MacFadyen, H.
1959	MacFadyen, H.
1960	MacFadyen, H.

"Bad-daraich" Salver

1960	Duncan, Tommy

John MacLean Cup

1924	Lamont, D.
1925	Lamont, D.
1926	Kennedy, H.
1927	Kennedy, H.
1928	Lamont, D.
1929	Kennedy, H.
1930	MacLean, D.
1931	MacLean, H.
1932	MacLean, H.
1933	Moss, G
1934	Simpson, W. J.
1935	McCallum, N.
1936	MacNab, A.
1937	Ross, D. F.
1938	MacFadyen, H.
1939	MacFadyen, H.
1948	Lawrie, R.
1949	MacFarquhar, P.
1950	MacFadyen, J.
1951	Campbell, A.
1952	Gillies, A.
1953	Gillies, A.
1954	MacDonald, R.
1955	MacFadyen, D.
1956	Lawrie, R.
1957	MacDonald, R.
1958	MacFadyen, H.
1959	MacDonald, K.
1960	MacDonald, K.

Duncan MacLeod Cup

1951	Burgess, J.
1952	Burgess, J.
1953	Burgess, J.
1954	None eligible
1955	MacFadyen, I.
1956	None eligible
1957	None eligible
1958	MacCallum, H.
1959	MacDonald, K.
1960	None eligible

Bobby MacLeod Cup

1960	Kenny Macintyre's Team

Cameron Cup

1930	Clark, D.
1931	Clark, D.
1932	MacIntyre, D.
1933	MacCallum, N. J.
1934	MacCallum, N. J.
1935	MacCallum, N. J.
1936	MacArthur, A.
1937	MacLean, C.
1938	MacDougall, N. M.
1939	Finlay, J.
1948	Connelly, J.
1949	MacDonald, J.
1950	MacDonald, J.
1951	MacDonald, J.
1952	MacDonald, J.
1953	MacFadyen, L.
1954	MacFadyen, L.
1955	MacRae, F.
1956	MacRae, F.
1957	Grant, G.
1958	Grant, G.
1959	MacAulay, R.
1960	Grant, G.

MacDonald Arms Cup

1950	Christie, A.
1951	MacIver, M.
1952	MacIver, C.
1953	Cowe, E. A.
1954	Carmichael, J. B.
1955	Tague, D.
1956	Bennett, A.
1957	Tague, D.
1958	MacKinnon, H.
1959	Bennett, A.
1960	MacFadyen, C. (Coll)

MacBrayne Cup

1953	MacKenzie, J. L.
1954	Jessiman, B.
1955	Buchanan, C.
1956	Forbes, A. F.
1957	Jessiman, B.
1958	Buchanan, C.
1959	Jessiman, B.
1960	Buchanan, C.

ERIC MACINTYRE

In the 1960s and 1970s spectators were fortunate enough to witness probably the greatest-ever rivalry in Highland Games history. Bill Anderson first competed in the games in 1958 and soon began eclipsing the records of George Clark and Edward Anderson. In 1963 Arthur Rowe, ex Olympic Games shot putter, came north and quickly learnt the skills of hammer throwing, weight over the bar and caber. All over Scotland, Bill and Arthur battled day after day during the games season, but always with a handshake at the end and on to the next event, often even travelling together. At Mull Highland Games Bill would interrupt a throwing event to come down in his hammer boots to the dancing platform to present a raffle prize or make the day for the winner of the children's race. It was a privilege to witness these two greats in action, but always with the old-fashioned word, sportsmanship, so often lacking in today's pampered stars.

Bill Anderson with the children of Bill MacCallum.

Bill with a typical trophy haul.

Arthur Rowe throwing the weight for distance.

It is easy to forget that there were many other fine heavy event athletes competing with Bill and Arthur, such as Gordon Forbes, Charles Simpson, and Charlie Allen. The latter would leave the heavy events and along with Rob Aitken, take off his kilt to come down the field and high jump. In 1961 John Freebairn, ex Partick Thistle goalkeeper, joined the Games circuit and the late Douglas MacNeilage spoke of how excited locals were that such a sportsman was coming to Mull Games. For the next decade and more John competed in all the heavy and jumping events with a strong, completive will, but always praising of the efforts of fellow competitors.

John Freebairn high jumping at Mull Games.

In the light events at that time there were many fine athletes. One such was the 1964 Powderhall Sprint winner Bill McLellan who was a fine all-round sprinter and jumper, setting a long jump record of 22ft 11ins in 1967. He was joined by other New Year Sprint winners such as Bob Swann, Bert Oliver and the great George McNeill who all sped down the Erray Park straight. In 1964 Ian Ward cleared 12ft 8ins in the pole vault using a steel pole. This was never beaten anywhere until fibre glass poles came in. The Glenn brothers, Sandy Nelson, Willie Rutherford and Willie Robertson excelled. Olympic finalist Alan Simpson from Rotherham set a half mile record in 1968 running in his bare feet. The MacBeath brothers from Caithness dominated the jumping events. James MacBeath excelled in both light and heavy events and brother Tom was the top middle distance runner on the circuit as well as a very competent jumper.

Local athletes such as Alistair MacNeill, Angus Macintyre Jnr, Bill McCallum and Duncan Macintyre took over from Gordon Grant. Bill McCallum recalls that he "made my debut aged 16 in the local events in 1964 but not successfully. I was hoping for a prize in the local high jump but the preceding event was a 440yds race in which I got caught by a flailing elbow at one of the tight bends and was still dazed for some time after." Two local names stand out from the 1960s and 1970s. Kenny Macintyre, son of Angus, excelled in sprint and jumps. In 1965 he cleared 48ft 7.5ins in the hop step and jump to beat Jay Scott's open record from 1953 and his father's local record which had stood since 1932. He set many local running records and in 1966 beat Allan Mann's long jump record from 1926. Kenny went on to become BBC Scotland's political correspondent and in the 1993 games programme wrote: "I doubt if anywhere on earth is a more stunningly beautiful setting for staging a sporting spectacular than Tobermory Games Field. Many of us who hold the Games dear, who regards Erray Park as hallowed turf, won't be able to attend today. But we'll be there in spirit." He died in 1999 aged 54 and is commemorated by a trophy in his name for the hop, step and jump.

A staged picture from 1965 with John Cameron measuring Kenny's hop, step record with Kenny and his father Angus.

ERIC MACINTYRE

Hailing from Lismore, Archie MacGillivray excelled in the middle distance running events, beating Gordon Grant's mile record and often winning the cross country race in memory of Alistair MacLachlainn. He came second in the half mile at Powderhall and showed great strength and courage over many races, often on hot afternoons.

Archie MacGillivray, Lismore, won the longer track races and the cross country.

Kenny Macintyre won the Chieftain's Cup for field events.

Archie and Kenny in 1967.

Left: Alan Simpson running barefoot at a Highland Games. Right: The 1971 Games with the Tiree Pipe Band on the march.

In Highland dancing the leading competitors were Jean Swanston, Rosemary MacGuire, Charlie Mill and Victor Wesley.

In piping Kenneth MacDonald, originally from Tiree, won the pibroch several times and was hard pressed by, among others, Arthur Gillies, Hector MacFadyen and William MacDonald.

From left: Iona MacAllister, Dawn Hickford, Mina Tague, Margaret Tague, Iona Tague (MacLean), Uilleam Tague, Islay Tague.

Lady Maclean and Games patrons in the 1960s.

Sir Lachlan Maclean and Iona MacLean, greatgranddaughter of Allan Mann, proudly displays her dancing trophy in 1998.

MULL HIGHLAND GAMES: THE CENTENARY

In 1965 Bill Clegg took over from Dr Tommy MacIntyre as the Tobermory GP. A Yorkshireman with an interest in athletics, he soon became involved in the Games and remained a judge for the next four decades. He donated a Clach (Gaelic for stone) and the prize money for a highly popular shot putt event.

Judge Bill Clegg in action.

Another judge in the heavy events for many years was Neil MacLean, known affectionately as "Derryguaig." He had been a heavy event competitor in his younger days and his distinctive deerstalker hat made him a kenspeckle figure on Games Day for many decades.

As Brian Robin prepares to throw the hammer, Bill Clegg and Derryguaig watch on.

By the mid 1970s the *King George* no longer plied the route to Staffa on Games Day and although a boat still brought spectators and customers from Oban direct to Tobermory, it really marked the end of an era.

Change was afoot on the Games Committee too. After Balachan's death Lorn Macintyre became Secretary for a few years, to be followed by Donnie Yule and Bert Laver, the latter a former convenor of dancing. In 1978 Colonel Charles A. MacLean passed away. A long-time Chairman and able Deputy Chieftain, the 1978 games programme said: "He led the ceremonial parade from the pier to the field and to the march he brought lustre, bearing and the dignified step of a Highland Officer of many campaigns in far-flung fields. Respected, indeed loved by all, we mourn the passing of a real Highland Gentleman of the old and noble school."

Mr Lorn Macintyre, games secretary; Mr Hugh Kain, clerk of the course, and the assistant clerk Mr Donald Kennedy.

Two views of a hot day at Mull games in 1969.

Dr MacLaren in the middle, his son on left and Major ("Scrap") Balfour Paul judge the dancing in 1967. "Scrap" had judged at Tobermory since the 1930s.

Mull Highland Games Since The 1980s

Like all events and organisations Mull Highland Games has witnessed changes in recent decades, but it is fair to say that its essential elements have remained the same. Patrons might now be called sponsors, trade stalls might now be found at Erray Park, but the competitions remain largely the same and people see the day as a major chance to catch up with friends and visiting family members. As Angus Macintyre wrote:

> "A respite from your labours
> A time of fun and laughs;
> The place to meet your neighbours
> In hearty Slainte –Vahs."

One of the major differences on Games Day itself is that boats no longer bring competitors and spectators direct to Tobermory from Oban, Coll, and Tiree. The ferry will come into Craignure and buses provide the onward transport to the Games. We have seen earlier how important was the arrival of the *King George* before the parade formed and was piped up to Erray Park. The parade now forms up at Ledaig and makes it way along main street and up the Back Brae as in former decades.

However, one of the things which has not changed is that the Games still has its characters and one of the most kenspeckle of recent decades was the late Ronnie Campbell from Bunessan. Ronnie was the commentator for many years at the games and brought his own stamp to that role. Craig Dunbar, the present commentator, writes: "I have to say a few words today on the passing of the legend that was Ronnie Campbell of Bunessan, Isle of Mull. I got to know him when I attended for the first time the Mull Highland Games back in the early years of this century when, perched aloft what looked like a fairly unsteady scaffolding commentary tower, Ronnie was regaling the crowds in Erray Park with all of the detail of what was going on down in the field and with stories of local history and more besides. His soft local accent added to the occasion and he engaged with the spectators and got them involved in every single event during the day. He carried out the same roles at both Inveraray and at the Argyllshire Gathering in Oban.

For many competitors and officials, Ronnie was Mull Games and every year we all looked forward to him invoking the crowd's support for what was always the hardest event on the card. For Ronnie, they all were! He knew everyone and everyone knew him. He was also the President for over 40 years of the Bunessan Show and was rightly made an MBE for all that he did to support and promote life on the island of Mull. I was more than happy to snatch the microphone from him that year and to announce that just award to the crowd who responded with tumultuous applause.

For all that life threw at him - and it was not always the kindest - Ronnie kept a totally positive approach to all that he did. In recent years he took more of a back seat at the Mull Games and was not there in person in 2017 but we all knew that that would have been a very difficult thing for him to do. I worked with him for a few years as secondary commentator and learned much from him about the art. He will be greatly missed and it is no exaggeration to say that his passing marks the end of an era.

Wallace McGowan a competitor for many years at the Games says the phrase "come on now ladies & gentlemen, bring them home, this is the hardest race on the card" for every race will always stay with me. Ronnie also ensured that the last competitor to cross the finish line (very often me in the scratch mile!) received a greater round of applause than the winner! A true legend & we'll ne'er see his like again. RIP Mr Mull Games."

Ronnie calls them home.

Craig Dunbar now fulfils the role of commentator in his own inimitable style, as he does at many Games all over Scotland. Craig is on the right in the picture, and handicapper Don Campbell on left.

Mull and Iona Pipe Band lead the parade.

A New Chieftain

As we have seen, Sir Charles MacLean often made heroic efforts to attend Mull Highland Games and this posed even greater challenges when he was appointed *Lord* Chamberlain to Queen Elizabeth II. On his death in 1990 his son, Sir Lachlan Hector Charles Maclean of Duart and Morvern, 12th Baronet, CVO, DL, succeeded him as Chief of Clan Maclean and Hereditary Chieftain of Mull Highland Games. He has performed his duties since then with the necessary blend of formality and humility, continuing his family's association with the Games stretching back to the 1930s.

Sir Lachan Maclean presents the Kenny Macintyre Memorial Cup to Tony Daffurn.

MULL HIGHLAND GAMES: THE CENTENARY

The Clan Maclean Association exists to co-ordinate Clan activities all over the world and in particular, to run the gatherings at Duart Castle. For a number of years the Association has had a presence at Mull Highland Games, welcoming Mac leans and their relatives from all over the world in the spirit of kinship. Indeed the Mull Highland Games could be said to be the "home" games of Clan MacLean.

Clan Maclean gather at Mull Highland Games.

The Engine Room Of The Games

We have seen earlier the important role which Hugh Kain played in Mull Highland Games and in the 1980s he returned for another dedicated time as Secretary. His daughter, Florence Kirsop acted as joint Secretary with Hugh until eventually assuming the role herself and filling it for the best part of thirty years. Her brother Andrew has been Chairman and now President of the Games Committee, thus carrying on a family role in organising Mull Highland Games for the vast majority of its 100 year history.

Sir Lachlan Maclean and Andrew Kain on Games Day.

Alongside the immense contribution of the Kain family stands the many decades of dedicated service given by their relatives, the MacLeod family. We have noted the legendary Bobby's piping and accordion roles, as well as his role as Chairman, and his son Robert succeeded him in that position. Another son Duncan served as Treasurer and mother Jean was an Assistant Secretary, as was Robert's daughter Joan Gunn.

Anne MacGregor worked alongside Angus Macintyre in the former Clydesdale Bank and has now taken on his mantle as Treasurer, a vital job in keeping the Games solvent.

Anne MacGregor and Florence Kirsop.

Judges And Officials

There is a strong tradition in the Highland Games that former competitors often go on to serve as judges and officials and Mull is no exception to this. In piping Hugh Kennedy and Hector MacLean competed in the 1930s and went on to judge in the 1960s and 1970s. They were succeeded by Iain MacFadyen and Ronnie Lawrie whose competitive record has been discussed earlier. In the heavy events Jock MacColl and Brian Robin were noted competitors before Jock took over as convenor, with Brian succeeding him on his death.

Jock MacColl and Brian Robin.

Bill MacCullum (left) and Robbie Carbury.

In the light events Bill MacCallum MBE was a gifted athlete of the 1960s and 1970s and is now Convenor. His dedication typifies the spirit of volunteering and he has pioneered events at the Games for younger athletes, a vital element of the continuity of the ancient tradition. Bill is pictured above on the left, busy as always on the fast moving field.

Bill recalls: "The 1980s was the decade when I stopped competing and started judging at the light events. Ronnie MacLean from Glenurquhart was a fellow judge. Ronnie travelled extensively on the Games circuit and was a big loss to the Games on his sudden death. Duncan MacIver was a stalwart, officiating at the jumps for many years until his sudden death. I recall the Bradley brothers from Staffin on Skye emerging as athletes excelling in both running and jumping events. Older brother Alasdair had a shorter career but Donald was still competing in 2022 in 800metres and mile races. I can only guess at what age he is now. Donald was an outstanding jumper and middle distance runner and has supported Mull Games for close to 40 years. In recent years both Donald and his son Ewen have been at Mull and Ewen himself is quite a performer and was awarded the title of the Scottish Highland Games Association (SHGA) "Athlete of the Year" in 2018.

ERIC MACINTYRE

Donald Bradley and son Ewan.

Bill MacCallum continues: "The 1990s were special for me as our younger son Stuart, who now judges with me, started competing and we travelled to many Games throughout Scotland for nearly 20 years. There was a lot of local [Argyll] talent at that time with Oban boys Keith Preston and Colin MacKenzie and John MacFadyen from Strachur. John still holds both the local and open mile record at Mull with 4minutes 31 seconds, a formidable time on the 6 laps with very tight bends to negotiate. My son Stuart excelled in the jumps and especially the triple jump and his main rivals were Donald Bradley, Mark Parham, Willie Stark and David Watson. David Watson was the man who broke the long standing triple jump record set by Tobermory's own Kenny MacIntyre in 1965, with a 49ft 4in leap.

Stephen King emerged as the top local and open heavy athlete at the end of the 1990s and still holds the ground records in both light and heavy hammers. Other accomplished heavies at the time were Bruce Aitken and Brian Robin. Brian continues to support Mull Games to the present day as the leading judge in the heavy events."

Bill records: "Over the years many runners have found the tight bends very challenging but 2 runners who had many successes at Mull were middle distance men Colin Welsh from Kelso and Matthew Turner from Campbeltown. I have known Matthew since he was 7 years old when he first competed in an indoor competition I organised in Campbeltown's Victoria Hall. I have to admit that what has given me the most pleasure at Mull is the fact that Mull Games has emerged as the top venue for jumping events in Scotland. Our Games have been awarded the RSHGA jumps championship for almost 10 years now and this has attracted some of Scotland's top jumpers. The Scottish championship has resulted in both the long jump and triple jump ground records also qualifying as the Scottish [RSHGA] records. Both records are held by Allan Hamilton from Edinburgh who is very likely to be at the 2023 Games. Allan's triple jump record of 50ft 1inch was set in 2016 but the long jump record and Scottish record has been bettered 4 times, starting with Allan's 24ft 6.5in in 2016 which lasted

2 years until Tony Daffurn from Coatbridge leapt 25ft 1in and then Tony extended the record to 25ft 3.5in in 2019 and then 2022 was the best of all with both Tony and Allan present and the friendly rivalry created another record with Allan clearing 25ft 5.5inches."

Allan Hamilton in action.

Tony Daffurn showing fine form.

Bill writes: "I feel very lucky to have had such a long association with Mull Games and I have to thank all the many committee members over all these years for allowing me the privilege of competing and then officiating. There are so many people I should have mentioned but space would not allow. I hope to continue judging for a few more years and then sit back and spectate from the banking opposite the long jump pit of course. I mentioned earlier the long standing high jump ground record set in 1955 by the great Jay Scott. My wish is that in my lifetime I can witness someone breaking this amazing record and I have a strong feeling this will happen sooner than later. Many thanks to Mull Highland Games for a lifetime of amazing memories."

Many others continue to help out in setting up the field, helping on the day with numerous tasks, not least the vital role of catering. The committee have purchased fixed-frame tents to replace the old marquees hired from Blacks of Greenock.

It is vital to feed the judges and officials.

An earlier catering team from the 1960s in the Aros Hall. From back left: Mrs Sproat, Betty Macintyre, Peggy Beaton, Betty MacPhail, Johan MacNeill, Mrs Henderson, Jeanie Tyrell. Front from left: Lexie MacNeill, Morag McGilp, Emily MacLean.

The Scottish Highland Games Association recognised the vital role of these volunteeers by presenting them with an award in 2017.

Alistair Maclean MBE, Bill MacCallum MBE and Alec Livingstone receive their awards.

Games programme covers over the years:

Programme
.. of ..
Mull Highland Games
1935

Chieftain, Captain Charles L. Maclean, R.N., Ballechin, Ballinluig.

Clerk of the Course, - - Malcolm MacLean, A.M.I.B.E.

Conveners of Field Committees, - { Rev. John M. Menzies. / A. M. McKenzie, Esq.

Steward of Piping and Dancing, - - Dugald MacQuarrie.

Judges of Piping and Dancing, - { John Macdonald, M.B.E. / Duncan McColl, Esq. / L. Balfour Paul, Esq.

Secretary, - - - - - - A. M. macLachlainn.

Treasurer, - - - - - J. M. Urquhart, J.P.

N.B.—
1. Only Judges, Competitors, and Stewards are allowed in the roped area.
2. On the Telegraph—
    (a.) The number of the Event is placed at the top of the board ;
    (b.) numbers are put up in the centre of the board immediately after each Event to indicate the Winners ;
    (c.) the Achievement is indicated on the lower part of the board.

Programme .. Two pence.

Sinclair & Paterson, Printers, Oban

PROGRAMME OF
MULL HIGHLAND GAMES
20th JULY, 1961

HEREDITARY CHIEFTAIN   Sir CHARLES HECTOR FITZROY MACLEAN, Bart., of Duart and Morvern

PRESIDENT - - - - - - - - - - A. H. ALLAN, Esq., of Linndhu

VICE-PRESIDENTS :

Col. C. P. ANDERSON of Mishnish

JOHN FORRESTER, Esq., of Ardnacross, Aros

Lt.-Col. CAMPBELL K. FINLAY of Ardow, Dervaig

Dr. R. FAWCITT, Glengorm Castle, Mull

G. S. GILLOTT, Esq., of Drimgigha, Dervaig

Col. BRUCE HARVEY of Kinloch

Miss ALICE HORSMAN of Drimnin, Morvern

Col. ERIC MACKENZIE, Calgary House, Mull

DONALD MACLEAN, Esq., Western Isles Hotel, Tobermory

Mrs ANNE M. MACLEOD, Gruinard, Tobermory

Dr. FLORA MACDONALD, Inverinate, Salen, Aros

Col. NIALL RANKIN, House of Treshnish, Mull

Chairman and Reception Convener - - - Provost CHAS. A. MACLEAN, Tobermory

---

Hon. Secretary - - - - - - - - - JOHN M. CAMERON
Hon. Treasurer - - - - - - - - - ANGUS MACINTYRE

FIELD COMMITTEE

Clerk of the Course	Hugh Kain
Commentator	John Parlett
Convener of Piping	Duncan Lamont
Convener and Steward of Dancing	Malcolm MacLean and Miss F. N. MacLean
Heavy Events—Convener	John MacDonald, Kilfinichen
Stewards	John MacQuarrie, Allan Cameron, John MacKechnie, Neil MacLean, Hugh Gillies, Bobby MacLean
Light Events—Convener	Angus Macintyre
Stewards	Ed. MacIntyre, Col. C. P. Anderson, A. L. Gardinor, J. D. Cameron, Cameron Whyte, M. McCorquodale
Official Starter	Doctor Lloyd, Glasgow
Official Timekeeper	Major Parker, Gruline
Documentation	D. A. Kennedy, A. MacMaster, Jack Bushell

MULL HIGHLAND GAMES

ERRAY PARK, TOBERMORY
(by kind permission of the Tobermory Golf Club)

Thursday 22nd July 2010

GAMES COMMENCE 10.30am Approx.

Souvenir
Programme
£2

Lucky
Number

215

ERIC MACINTYRE

Mull Highland Games
Tobermory Isle of Mull
July 22,1971
PROGRAMME

HEREDITARY CHIEFTAIN	LORD MACLEAN OF DUART AND MORVERN
PRESIDENT	Colonel CHARLES A. MACLEAN
CHAIRMAN	Provost A.R.C. MACLEOD, Tobermory
VICE-CHAIRMAN	John MACKECHNIE, Esq., Tobermory

VICE-PRESIDENTS

A.H. Allan, Esq., of Linndhu
Allan Cameron, Esq., Linlithgow
John Forrester, Esq., of Ardnacross
Richard S. Forrester, Esq., Western Isles Hotel
A.L. Gardinor, Esq., of Mishnish
G.S. Gillott, Esq., of Drimgigha

Miss Alice Horsman of Drimnin
Dr Flora MacDonald, Salen
Col. Eric MacKenzie of Calgary
Donald MacLean, Esq., Clansman Rest.
Major L. Balfour Paul of Quinish
Alexander Yule, Esq., Tobermory

JOINT HON. SECRETARIES: Alexander MacLean
Hugh Kain

HON. TREASURER: Angus Macintyre

FIELD COMMITTEE

Clerk of the Course	Hugh Kain
Track and Field Referees	A.L. Gardinor, Dr W. Clegg
Convener of Piping	Duncan MacQuarrie, Jnr., M.A., Dip. Ed.
Stewards of Piping	Allan Beaton, D.M. MacQuarrie, M.A.
Convener of Dancing	Albert Laver, Oban
Conveners of Heavy Events	J. MacKechnie, John MacDonald
Assistants	Major F. Parker, J. McQuarrie, Neil MacLean, Bobby MacLean
Convener of Light Events	Alex. Yule
Assistants	Ian Anderson, Lorne MacIntyre, J. Farquharson, D.M. Yule, J.D. McNeilage, Rear Admiral H. H. Hughes, J. McDonald
Official Starter	Robert Campbell, Alexandria
Quartermaster	Alex. J. Noble
Programmes	Mrs D.A. Kennedy and Miss MacDougall
Convener of Raffle for Tregnum	Mrs A. MacNeill

ACKNOWLEDGEMENTS: The Games Committee wish to record their grateful thanks to all local voluntary workers who gave their time in the preparation of the field.

FREE GIFT DRAW: Tickets available on Field for Draw. Prize: One Tregnum 'Long John' whisky, kindly donated by Long John Distilleries Ltd.

The Isle of Tiree Pipe Band will lead the parade and give selections on the field throughout the day.

Lunches with beer, teas, lemonade and other light refreshment available on field.

Event times are approximate.

MULL HIGHLAND GAMES
TOBERMORY ISLE OF MULL

THURSDAY, 20th. JULY, 1978
Commencing at 11. 30 am

PROGRAMME

HEREDITARY CHIEFTAIN   LORD MACLEAN OF DUART AND MORVERN

PRESIDENT

CHAIRMAN   A.R.C. MACLEOD, TOBERMORY

VICE CHAIRMAN   ALEXANDER YULE, TOBERMORY

Honorary Treasurer   Angus Macintyre

Honorary Secretary   Albert E. Laver

Clerk of Course   Hugh Kain

Official Starter   Kenneth Macintyre

Official Recorder   Henry H. Hughes

oOo

OBAN PIPE BAND
WILL LEAD THE PARADE AND PLAY SELECTIONS ON GAMES FIELD

oOo

PROGRAMME   10 PENCE.

The Events Since 1980

The traditional events in dancing, piping, heavy and light athletics have endured over the century-long history of Mull Highland Games, but there have been changes in recent decades. Events for young athletes have been added to the programme, but more family-friendly elements are now included. The ever-popular children's races are held, along with kiltie dashes and visitors' races.

In the 1980s a second English heavy event athlete and former Olympian, Geoff Capes, came north to the Highland Games circuit and had many battles with the great Bill Anderson who was by now nearing the end of his illustrious career. In 2023 the leading heavy event athletes include Kyle Randalls, Sinclair Patience, Scott Hutchison and Vlad Tulacek.

The children race to the finishing line.

The visitors race round the tight bottom bend.

Oban High School Pipe Band under Pipe Major Angus MacColl.

Wallace McGowan rounds the tight bend to the finishing straight.

Angus MacPhail from Skipinnish in action.

Conclusion

Hopefully, this short work has given a flavour of the rich history of Mull Highland Games since its formal foundation in 1923 and the smaller events which took place over the past 150 years. It has not sought to cover all events or people, competitors and officials, but rather to highlight important developments and "characters" in the history of the Games. At the very least the work can form the basis for future ancestral and historical research on this wonderful event, as people compile their family trees and plot where relatives fitted into the Mull Games picture. For one hundred years competitors, spectators, officials and judges have made their way to Erray Park, a most wonderful, natural arena, for, as Angus Macintyre put it:

> "The great seas number seven
> And I've sailed them in my day
> But there's nowhere nearer Heaven
> Than Tobermory Bay."

Here's to people climbing the Back Brae for many decades to come.

ERIC MACINTYRE

About the author

Eric Macintyre was brought up in Tobermory and first officiated at Mull Highland Games aged 13. He had a long career in higher education and was awarded the MBE for his work. He has written extensively on sport and general historical topics. He has a collection of archival material on the history of Highland Games and has drawn heavily on it for this book.

Printed in Poland
by Amazon Fulfillment
Poland Sp. z o.o., Wrocław
09 July 2023

22a154f9-1fe0-42b0-8fac-36c52718e0e1R01